Learn to do Redwork

Contents

Redwork, an Historical Appreciation

by Rita Weiss

My romance with Redwork began at a charming exhibit on Redwork mounted by Laurene Sinema of the Quilted Apple in Phoenix, Arizona and her friends at the 1998 International Quilt Festival in Houston, Texas. Since then, I have become a confirmed Redwork devotee.

Those simple outline stitches on the Redwork in that first exhibit triggered hidden memories of my own childhood.

A small bed, covered with what I now know was a Redwork coverlet, occupied one of the bedrooms in my aunt's house. During my childhood the cousins would pour into that back room, attempting to be the first one to locate a design that might be identified as coming from a favorite story or book.

Perhaps it was the desire to return to those carefree youthful days that set me on a quest to own a Redwork quilt and learn more about this delightful technique. Finding a Redwork quilt given today's internet auction capabilities was easy. Redwork quilts were found, ordered, and delivered to my office and met with an approving chorus from our entire staff. Everyone wanted to pick the block of her choice. When the chorus of "I can make one like that" rippled through the building, I realized that we had to share my Redwork quilts with more than just our staff.

And so, this book was born.

We have taken blocks from my old-time quilts and presented them in a form which will enable you to copy them for your own quilts. In addition, we've given you instructions on how to do the simple embroidery, and we've included some examples of quilts that we made using the blocks. The blocks in a favorite old quilt photographed on the next page, were put together in a traditional Redwork style which was to feather stitch them together with red thread in a style reminiscent of a crazy quilt. In keeping with that theme, one of our staff created a Redwork crazy quilt for me and my three daughters called the "Weiss Women Crazy Quilt" which appears on the back cover.

Because I find quilt history so fascinating, I set forth also to learn more about the history of Redwork, how it evolved and to trace its popularity.

Luckily, there is a group of quilters today called The American Quilt Study Group (AQSG) who also find the history of quilting fascinating. This group is a non-profit organization devoted to the finding and dissemination of the history of quiltmaking as a significant art of women. Membership and participation are open to all interested persons. If you are interested, write to them at:

The American Quilt Study Group
P. O. Box 4737
Lincoln, NE 68504-0737

Yearly the AQSG publishes the research papers which are presented at their annual seminar in their publication called "Uncoverings." They were able to start me on my quest.

In 1876, the Centennial Exhibition in Philadelphia introduced the Aesthetic Movement to America. Started in England in the 1860's under William Morris, this movement stressed that whatever made the home more attractive, more beautiful and more useful was important. Traditional patchwork quilts were frowned upon whereas beautiful surface embroidery was considered proper. Women were encouraged to literally paint with thread and to create their own embroidery designs. Although the ideal was original art work, copying designs created by artists became acceptable.

The Royal School of Art Needlework in Kensington, England had a very popular display at the Exhibition. It included embroidered bedspreads with beautiful designs based on medieval Renaissance designs. A few years later, Harper's Bazaar began to publish these designs from the Royal School. The designs were printed in black outlines, and the embroiderer was to make her own choices as to which colors to use and where to shadow her designs. Many women, however, chose merely to follow the outline using either a stem or outline stitch. This type of stitching came to be known as Kensington-stitch Embroidery.

These designs were deemed suitable for bed quilts especially for children. The definition of a quilt during this time is not exactly the definition that we would have today. Virginia Gunn in her article in the 1984 edition of Uncoverings, quotes an 1879 magazine which says:

> "A quilt means, properly speaking, something quilted—i.e. wadded and sewn down...In these days, and with a decorative end in view, such very elaborate work hardly repays the time spent on it; but the coverlet is to be recommended as an excellent object for work and design. Outline work in one color is very suitable for this purpose..."

While the author of the above was probably speaking of a coverlet completely embroidered in one magnificent piece, many quilters preferred to follow their traditional quilt-making methods even though this patchwork technique was frowned upon by the taste makers. Each block was embroidered on a separate patch, and the patches sewn together to create a quilt. My special Redwork quilt pictured is such a quilt. Each block was done individually, and then the quilt was put together in crazy quilt style.

Most of these outline quilts were intended for children, making it necessary to use a material that would survive many washings. They were therefore worked most often with a cotton Turkey Red embroidery floss, which was the most colorfast color available. For those of us who live in an era when anything made with red dye must be pre-washed and pre-washed to eliminate running, the fact that a red dye was considered colorfast seems strange.

The color known as Turkey Red was probably developed in the 17th century. Although some historians believe that Turkey Red was developed by Indian dyers because there were such dyes in India before the first century, Turkey Red is generally thought to have developed in the area around Turkey. The process was so complicated that it required over four

months for completion, and it took more than 100 years for other countries to duplicate the process. Turkey Red was an expensive process, but it never bled, and it lasted forever. Even after it was finally duplicated, the entire process was never really revealed. By 1940, synthetic dyes had taken over the market place, and red dye became the problem it is to this day. Although other cotton colors, especially blues, were considered colorfast during this period, Turkey Red was the cotton thread of choice for outline work. Threads dyed with the Turkey Red process were advertised with the Turkey Red logo, a large turkey with the word RED stamped across his chest.

Quilts made in the Kensington stitch remained popular well into the twentieth century. In addition to being used as children's quilts, many of these quilts were used as friendship

quilts with each block embroidered by a separate maker. This was perhaps how my antique quilt was made. Often the blocks were embroidered on recycled flour or sugar sacking. The designs were also used to make dresser scarves and pillow covers.

For many years during the first part of the twentieth century, the designs could be purchased preprinted onto muslin squares, called "penny squares" because they sold for a penny each. In addition, many stores sold the designs as perforated patterns which could be stamped upon a block by "pouncing" stamping powder or even cinnamon through the holes in the pattern. For many quilters, however, the best way to obtain their patterns was the traditional method used since the 1860's: they traced the designs from the magazines of the era.

Whatever the medium, outline designs often depicted state birds, state flowers, animals and nursery rhyme characters. Since there were no effective copyright laws during this period, designs for outline embroidery could be printed with impunity. Especially popular were the designs of Kate Greenaway, a famous artist of the period. Greenaway was especially known for her little girls in Victorian dresses—so popular that even today little girls' dresses are created in the Greenaway style.

Today many of the same designs appear in old Redwork Quilts, table linens, dresser scarves and pillows, and many of them are reproduced here. I hope that you will share my enthusiasm for Redwork and use the designs in this book to create your own Redwork quilts.

Learn to do Redwork

Supplies

Fabric

Use good quality 100% cotton fabrics for your redwork quilts. We used unbleached muslin for the embroidery, but any white or off-white high-quality cotton fabric can be used.

Pre-washing your fabric is recommended, but not absolutely necessary. If you choose not to pre-wash, you must test the fabric to make sure that it is colorfast and pre-shrunk. Start by cutting a 2"-wide strip (cut crosswise) of each fabric you have selected for your quilt. To determine whether the fabric is colorfast, immerse each strip separately into a clean bowl of extremely hot water, or hold the fabric strip under hot running water. If your fabric bleeds a great deal, all is not necessarily lost. You might be able to wash all of that fabric until all of the excess dye has washed out. Fabrics which continue to bleed after they have been washed several times should be eliminated. You do not want your red fabrics bleeding onto the embroidered squares.

To test for shrinkage, take each saturated strip and iron it dry with a hot iron. When the strip is completely dry, measure and compare it to your original length. If all of your fabric strips shrink about the same amount, then you really have no problem. When you wash your finished quilt, you may achieve the puckered look of an antique quilt. If you do not want this look, you will have to wash and dry all of the fabric before beginning so that shrinkage is no longer a problem. If only one of your fabrics is shrinking more than the others, it will have to be eliminated.

Needles

There are several different types and sizes of needles that can be used for embroidery. Sharps, sizes 7 to 10, are popular, but embroidery needles, sizes 8 and 7, are recommended because the eye of the needle is longer for easier threading. We used size 8 embroidery needles, but you should use the size and type of needle you are comfortable with to do your embroidery.

Embroidery Floss

Six-strand cotton embroidery floss was used to embroider the designs in our Redwork quilts. Work with two strands in 18" lengths. For the redwork, choose a shade of red such as Anchor #47 or DMC #498.

Embroidery Hoops

The best embroidery results are achieved when using an embroidery hoop to hold the fabric taut while stitching. There are several types and sizes of hoops available on the market. Wooden hoops with an adjustable screw are the most common, but there are also spring hoops and the newer Q-snaps™. Use the type and size hoop you find most comfortable for embroidering. It is best to use a hoop that is larger than the design you are embroidering.

Redwork Embroidery

Tracing the Design

Cut muslin into the size specified with the quilt instructions.

Center muslin over the design and trace using a sharp lead pencil or fabric marking pen or pencil. If you use a fabric pen, be sure to follow the manufacturer's directions for proper use. If you cannot see the lines clearly, use a light box for tracing.

Embroidering the Design

Wash hands before you start your hand embroidery to avoid soiling the redwork muslin. Thread floss into needle; do not tie a knot in end.

To begin stitching, come up from wrong side of fabric, leaving a 1" tail. Hold the thread end in place so that it is overcast with the first few stitches that are made. Cut the excess thread close to your work.

Another way to begin stitching is to weave thread through several stitches on the wrong side of your work first.

As you embroider separate lines in a close area, it is best to carry the thread across the back as long as the distance is not more than 1". If the lines are more than an inch apart, weave thread through a few stitches on the back.

Never carry thread across an unworked area.

When finished stitching, weave thread through several stitches on the back and cut away excess thread.

THE STITCHES

The main stitch that was used to outline the designs was the **Stem Stitch, Fig 1.** Bring the needle up at 1. Hold thread down with the thumb of your non-stitching hand. Reinsert needle at 2 and bring up at 3, about halfway between 1 and 2. Pull the thread through and continue in this manner with thread held below stitching line and working from left to right.

Fig 1

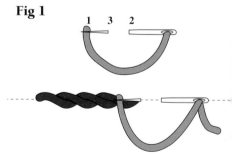

The **Satin Stitch**, **Fig 2**, was used sparingly to fill in small enclosed areas. Come up at 1 and down at 2. Continue with Straight Stitches very close together to fill desired pattern.

Fig 2

The **Backstitch**, **Fig 3**, was used to cover tight curves and can also be used to outline your designs if you desire.

Fig 3

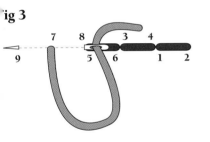

Bring needle up at 1, a stitch length away from beginning of design line. Stitch back down at 2, at beginning of line. bring needle up at 3, then stitch back down to meet previous stitch at . Continue in this manner, working in a right to left direction.

The **Straight Stitch**, **Fig 4**, was used to cover small straight lines. Come up at 1 and down at 2. Straight Stitches can be varying sizes and spaced regularly or irregularly.

Fig 4

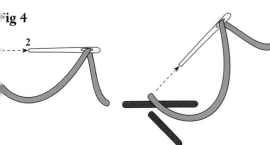

French Knots, **Fig 5**, were used for eyes, strawberry specks, and any other place where a small dot was needed. Bring needle up at 1. Wrap thread once around shaft of needle. Insert point of needle at 2 (close to, but not into 1). Hold knot down as you pull needle through to back of fabric.

Fig 5

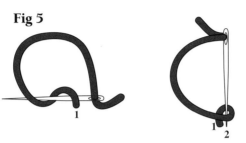

The Weiss Women Crazy Quilt, back cover, was embellished with the **Feather Stitch**, **Fig 6**, along the seams of the pieced blocks. Come up at 1 and go down at 2 (to left of and even with 1); emerge at 3 (below and between 1 and 3) with top of needle over thread. Pull thread completely through and go down at 4; emerge at 5 (below 3 and 4 and directly under 1). Pull thread completely through and continue stitching in same manner. End by making a small stitch over last loop.

Fig 6

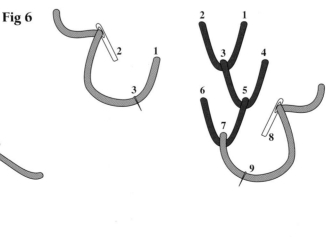

Finishing the Embroidered Block

When embroidery is completed, wash in cool water if soiled. To press, place block face down on a hard, padded surface (ironing board with terry towel works fine); press carefully.

Trim block to measurement specified in individual quilt instructions, being sure to center the design. To do this, find the approximate center of the design and measure an equal distance to all four sides. For example, if the block is to be cut at 6 1/2" square, measure 3 1/4" from the center point to each side and trim. A wide acrylic ruler and a rotary cutter will aid in measuring and cutting.

Redwork Designs

The 77 re-creations of Antique Blocks are found on pages 7 to 45. Use them in your own quilt designs or be inspired to make one of our four quilts (and also a pillow) photographed on the front and back cover. Instructions for the quilts and pillow follow on pages 46 to 58.

Child's Comfort Irish Chain Designs

Circus Elephant

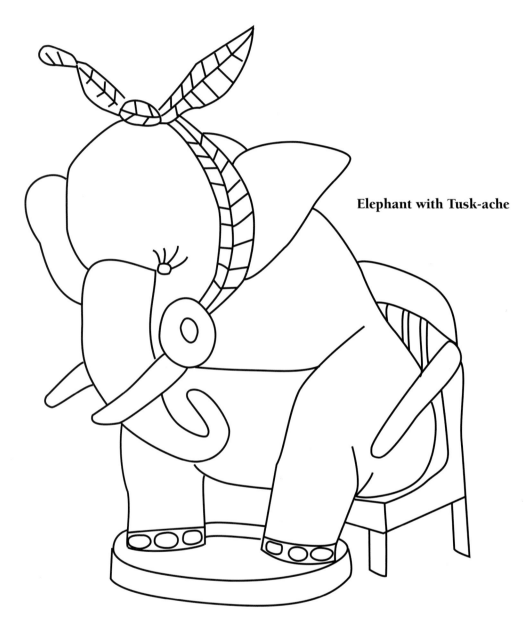

Elephant with Tusk-ache

Frog with Umbrella

Owl Couple

9

Dancing Pig

Bulldog Dressed Up

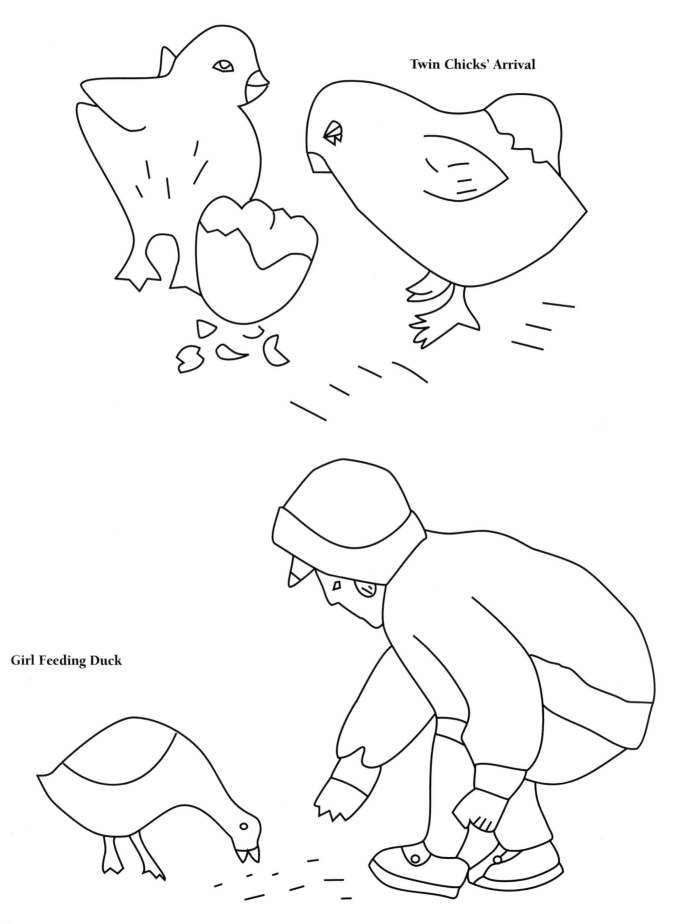

Twin Chicks' Arrival

Girl Feeding Duck

Happy Hen

Pony

13

Harried Hare

Bunny Tail-side

Rooster

Dallying Duck

Cow at Trough

Smiling Cat

Dog at Home

Ruby Red Log Cabin Designs

Cameo Girl

Harnessed Horse

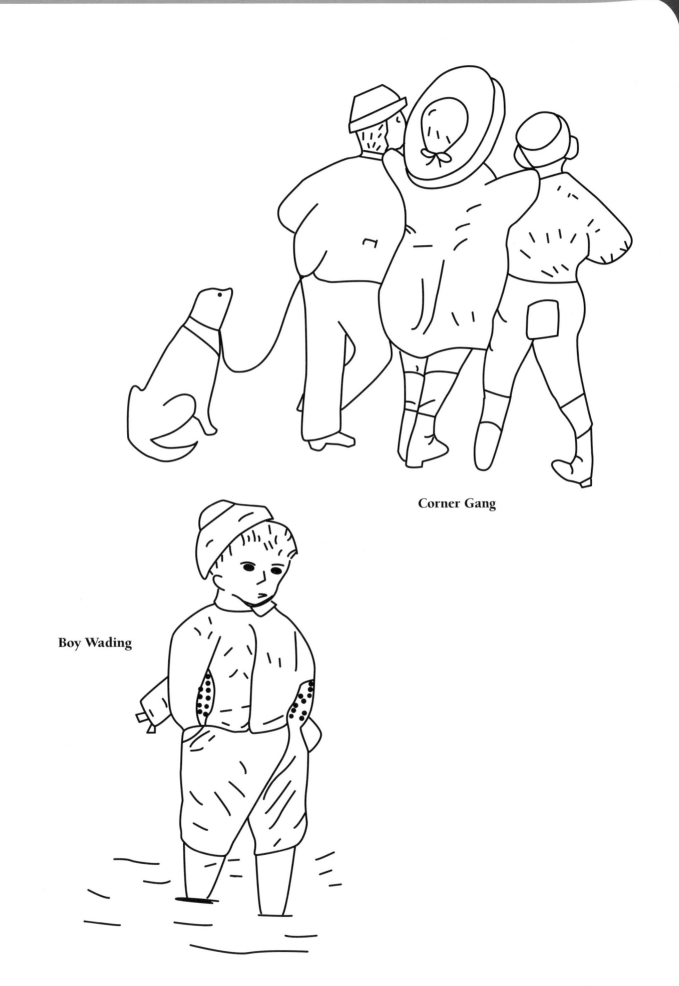

Corner Gang

Boy Wading

Setter

Sailor Gal

Sewing Lesson

Pensive Lady

Hoot Owl

Baseball Trio

Veiled Maiden

Boy in Cameo

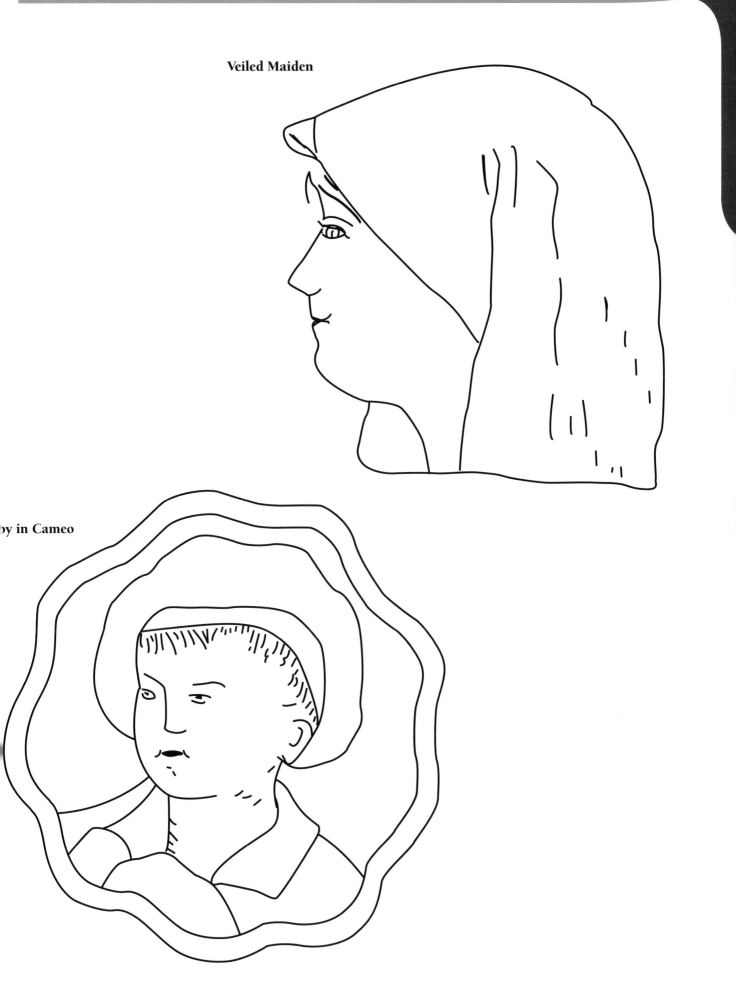

Country Boy

Chained Bull

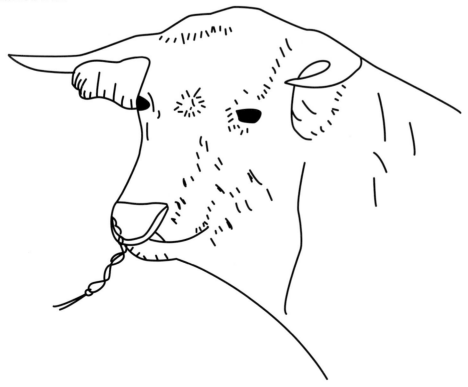

Uncle Sam

Muzzled Puppy

Victorian Girl

Chicks in Wooden Shoe

Kickball Boy

Lady with Turban

Mad Dogs

Dutchman Toast

Lady Perched in Tree

Darlin' Dress Up

Sunshine Toddler

Dutch Girls

29

Crabby Child

Easter Parade

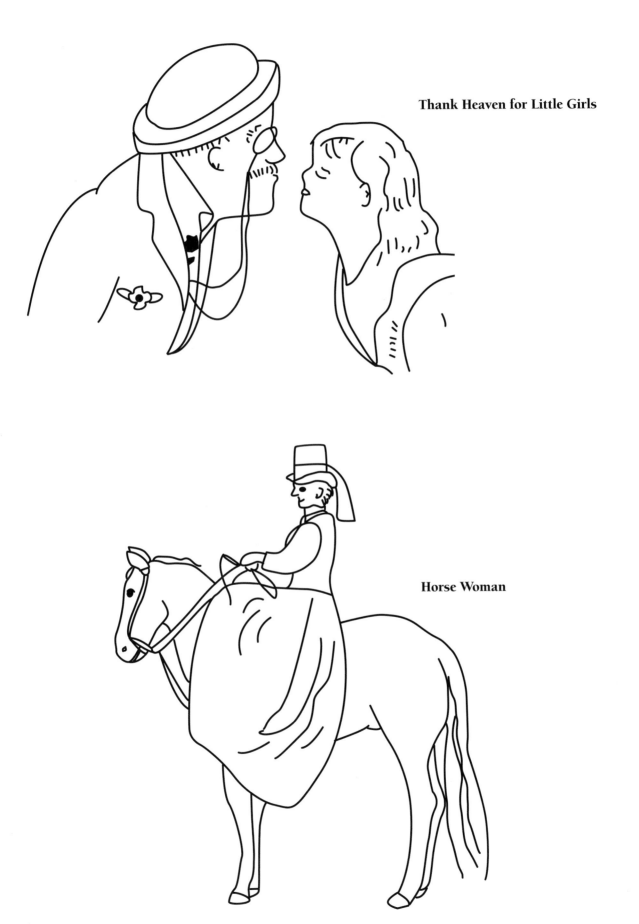

Thank Heaven for Little Girls

Horse Woman

General Washington

Child with Ouch

Kitty and Basket

Little Old Lady

Maid with Duster

Genteel Garden Quilt Designs

Cherries

Basket of Strawberries

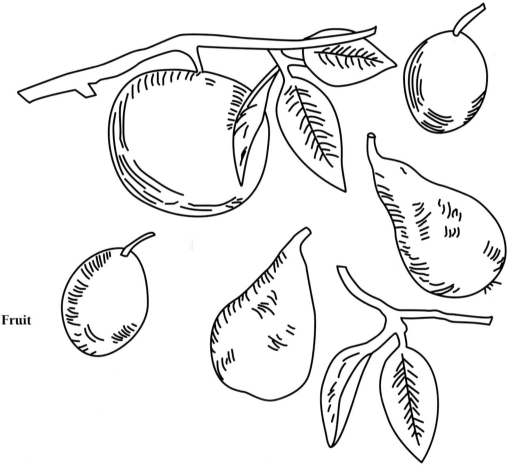

Bunch o' Fruit

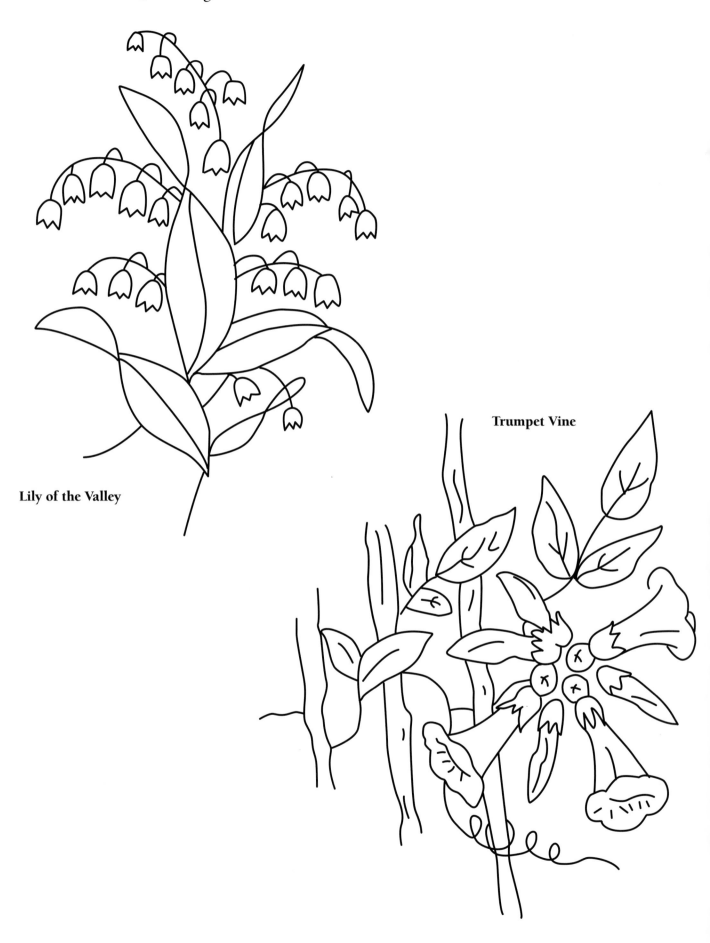

Lily of the Valley

Trumpet Vine

Nesting bird

Fall Vine

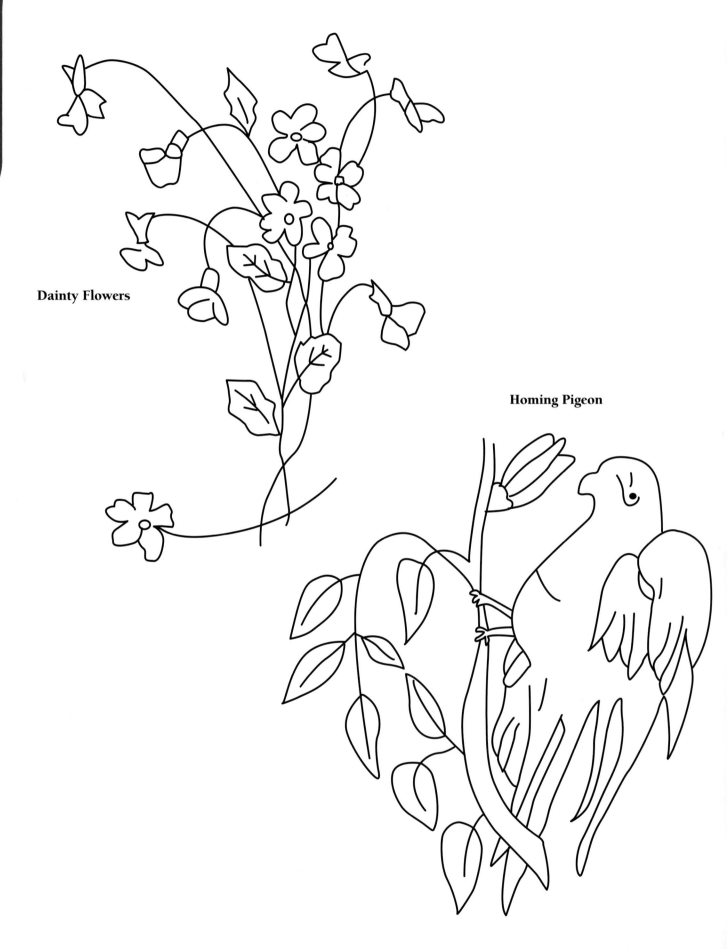

Dainty Flowers

Homing Pigeon

Iris Bouquet

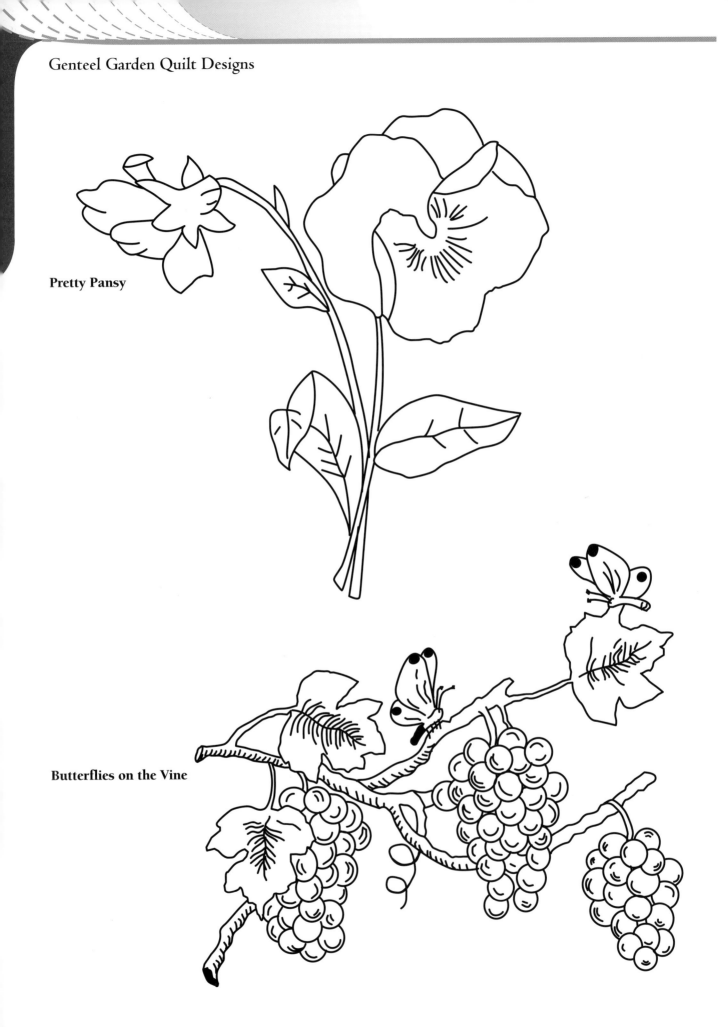

Pretty Pansy

Butterflies on the Vine

Calla Lily

Cyclamen

41

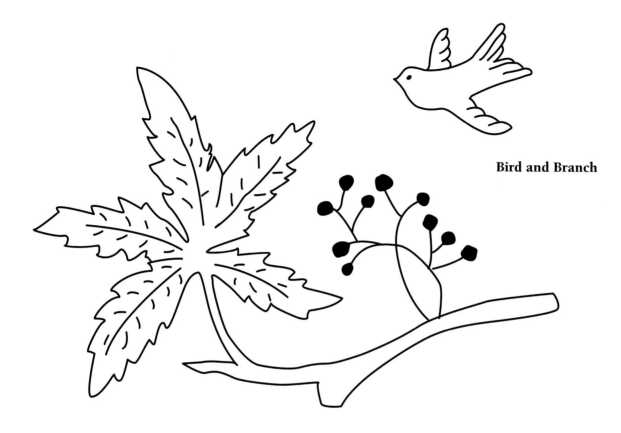

Bird and Branch

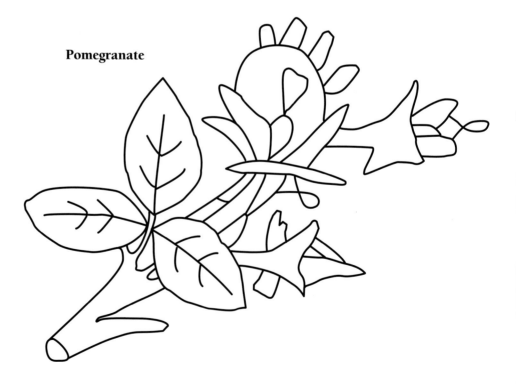

Pomegranate

Cherry Branch

Butterfly

Dainty Daisies

Glamour Pose

Little Lady with Turban

Little Sailor Gal

Small Pensive Lady

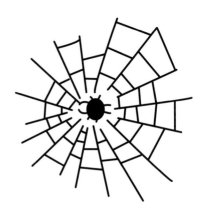

Spider Web

Ruffled Pillow Design

Baby with Mirror

Child's Comfort Irish Chain

Approximate Size:
45" x 60"

Finished Block Size:
7¹/₂" square

Materials

1¹/₄ yds muslin (Block A - embroidered blocks)

1 yd total assorted lt red prints (Block B)

1³/₄ yds dk red print (Block B, second border, binding)

¹/₄ yd tone on tone muslin print (Block B)

³/₈ yd lt red print (first border)

2³/₄ yds backing fabric
dk red embroidery floss
batting

Cutting Requirements

Cut the following:

17 - 9" squares, muslin (Block A)

nine 2"-wide strips, dk red print (Block B)

12 - 2"-wide strips, assorted lt red prints (Block B)

four 2"-wide strips, tone on tone muslin print (Block B)

68 - 2" squares, lt red print (Block A)

five 2"-wide strips, lt red print (first border)

ten 2¹/₂"-wide strips, dk red print (second border and binding)

Embroidery Patterns
(pages 7 to 17)

Quilt Lay

Instructions

Making the Quilt Blocks

BLOCK A

1. Trace a pattern, centered, onto each muslin square.

2. Embroider designs referring to Learn to do Redwork, pages 4 and 5.

3. Trim embroidered blocks to 7½" square.

4. Place a 2" lt red square in corner of embroidered square with right sides together, **Fig 1.**

Fig 1

5. Sew diagonally from corner to corner of 2" square, **Fig 2.**

Fig 2

Hint: For easier sewing, draw a line from corner to corner on wrong side of 2" square and sew on drawn line.

6. Repeat steps 4 and 5 at remaining corners, **Fig 3.**

Fig 3

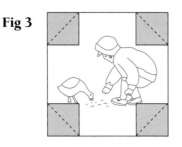

7. Trim corners ¼" from stitching, **Fig 4.**

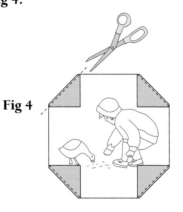

Fig 4

8. Press corners back to complete Block A, **Fig 5.**

Fig 5

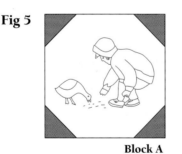

Block A

9. Repeat steps for remaining Block A.

BLOCK B

1. Sew strips together in strips sets as shown, **Fig 6.** Press seams for rows 1, 3 and 5 in one direction and rows 2 and 4 in opposite direction.

Fig 6

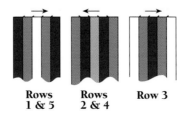

Rows 1 & 5   Rows 2 & 4   Row 3

2. Cut across strip sets at 2" intervals, **Fig 7.**

Fig 7

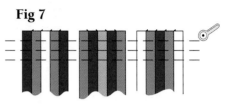

3. Sew strips together in rows, **Fig 8.** Repeat for a total of 18 Block B.

Fig 8

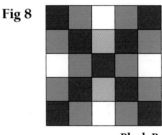

Block B

Making the Quilt Top

1. Place blocks according to quilt layout.

2. Sew blocks together in rows; press seams in alternating directions.

3. Sew rows together.

4. Press quilt top carefully.

5. Refer to Adding Borders, page 61, and sew borders to quilt top.

6. Press quilt top carefully.

Finishing the Quilt

Refer to General Directions, pages 62 to 64, to mark, layer, quilt and bind your quilt.

Photographed quilt was quilted diagonally through the dk red squares and in the ditch around the embroidered squares.

Ruby Red Log Cabin

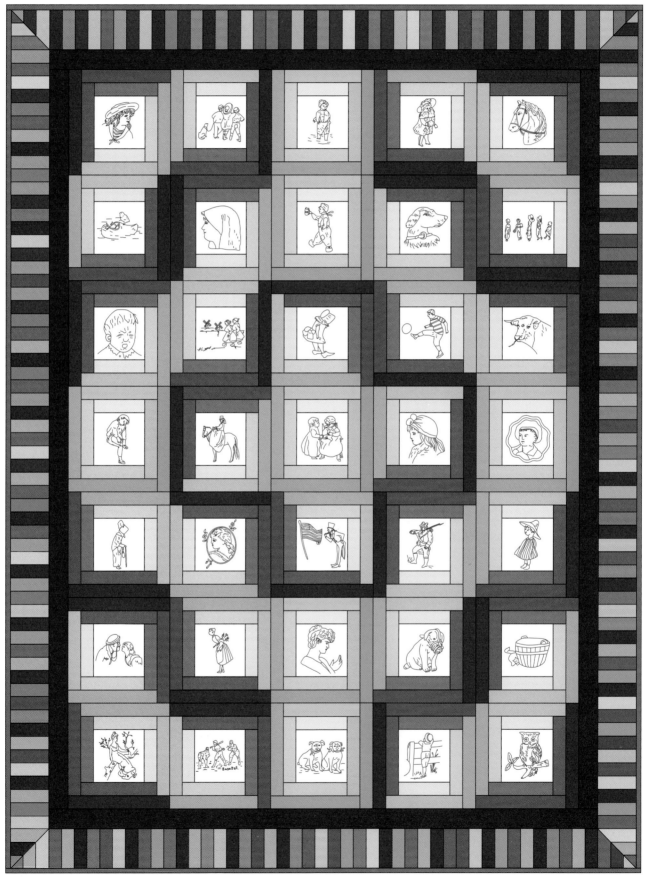

Quilt Layout

Approximate Size:
2 1/2" x 96 1/2"

Finished Bock Size: 12" square

Materials

. yds muslin (embroidery)
. 1/2 yds assorted dk red prints (blocks
  and second border)
. yds assorted lt red prints (blocks
  and second border)
. 1/4 yd dk red print (1st border)
. 1/4 yd med red print (binding)
. 1/2 yds backing fabric
. win-size batting
. ed embroidery floss

Cutting Requirements

. Cut 35 - 8" squares of muslin for
mbroidery.

. For "logs," cut dk and lt red fabrics
nto 2"-wide strips, then cut:

35 - 2" x 6 1/2" strips, lt red prints
42 - 2" x 8" strips, lt red prints
42 - 2" x 9 1/2" strips, lt red prints
42 - 2" x 11" strips, lt red prints
28 - 2" x 8" strips, dk red prints
28 - 2" x 9 1/2" strips,
    dk red prints
28 - 2" x 11" strips, dk red prints
28 - 2" x 12 1/2" strips,
    dk red prints
7 - 2" x 12 1/2" strips, lt red prints

Note: You will have strips left
over from step 1 to use later for
the second border.

. For first border, cut eight 2 1/2"-
wide dk red strips, then refer to
inishing the Quilt, page 61 when
uilt blocks are sewn together.

. For binding, cut ten 2 1/2"-wide
trips from med red print.

Embroidery Patterns
(pages 18 to 33)

Instructions

Making the Quilt Blocks

1. Trace a pattern onto each muslin
square.

2. Embroider designs referring to
Learn to Redwork, pages 4 and 5.

3. Trim embroidered blocks to 6 1/2"
square.

4. Place embroidered blocks in seven
rows of five blocks across.

5. Pin a numbered tag to each block
to keep track of position, **Fig 1**. Keep
tags on blocks until quilt top is finished.

Fig 1

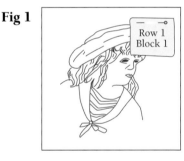

Note: There are five different
blocks based on positioning of
the dark and light red strips, **Fig
2**. You will need seven of each
block. Follow quilt layout (page
48) to make correct block for cor-
responding position in the layout.

Fig 2

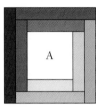

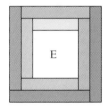
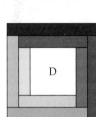

6. For Block A, sew a 2" x 6 1/2" lt red
print strip to bottom edge of embroidered block, **Fig 3**; press seam toward
outside edge, **Fig 4**.

Fig 3

Fig 4

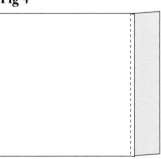

continued next page

49

Ruby Red Log Cabin

7. Turn block clockwise a quarter turn and sew a 2" x 8" lt red strip to embroidered block, **Fig 5**; press seam toward outside edge.

Fig 5

8. Turn block again and sew a 2" x 8" dk red strip to block, **Fig 6**; press seam toward outside edge.

Fig 6

9. To finish the first round, sew a 2" x 9¹/2" dk red strip to block, **Fig 7**; press seam toward outside edge.

Fig 7

10. Continue adding strips in same manner to complete second round, **Fig 8.**

11. Make Blocks B, C and D in the same manner, noting that the starting place is different with each block, **Fig 9**. Continue adding strips in order, turning block a quarter turn after sewing each strip.

Fig 9

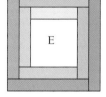

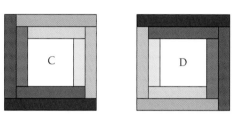

12. Make Block E in the same manner using only lt red fabrics, **Fig 10.**

Fig 10

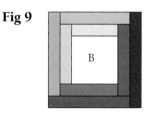

Fig 8

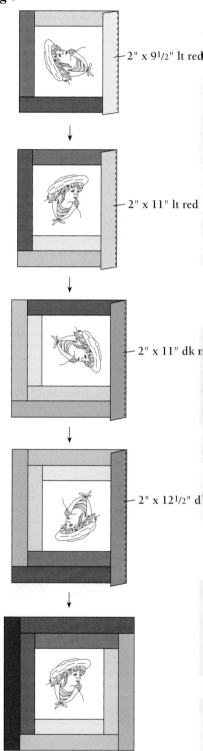

2" x 9¹/2" lt red

2" x 11" lt red

2" x 11" dk r

2" x 12¹/2" d

Making the Quilt Top

1. Position blocks according to numbered tags.

2. Sew blocks together in pairs, then sew pairs together, **Fig 11.** Press quilt top carefully.

3. Refer to Adding Borders, page 61, to sew first border to quilt top.

continued next page

Fig 11

Ruby Red Log Cabin

4. For pieced second border, sew left-over 2"-wide strips together randomly; sew in sets of six to eight strips, **Fig 12.** Press seams in one direction.

Fig 12

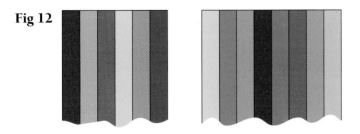

5. Cut across strip sets at 4¹/₂" intervals, **Fig 13.**

Fig 13

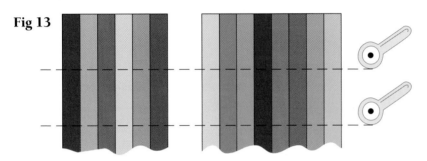

6. Measure quilt top lengthwise and crosswise. Sew strips together to make two border strips for each measurement adding 8¹/₂" to each strip to allow for mitering, **Fig 14.**

Fig 14

7. Refer to Adding Borders with Mitered Corners, page 62, to attach border.

8. Press quilt top carefully.

Finishing the Quilt

Refer to General Directions, pages 62 to 64 to mark, layer, quilt and bind your quilt.

The photographed quilt was quilted in the ditch around each block and between borders.

Genteel Garden Quilt

Embroidery Patterns
(pages 34 to 42)

Foundation Pattern (page 54)
Sashing Strip

Instructions

Making the Blocks

1. Trace a pattern, centered, onto each muslin square.

2. Embroider designs referring to Learn to do Redwork, pages 4 and 5.

3. Trim embroidered blocks to 6$\frac{1}{2}$" square.

Making the Sashing Strips

Note: The sashing strips in this quilt are foundation pieced.

1. Trace Sashing Strip pattern onto foundation as described in Tracing the Block, page 59. You will need 40 foundations.

2. See Making a Foundation-Pieced Block, pages 60 to 61, to piece the sashing strips, **Fig 2**. Trim sashing strips to 2$\frac{1}{2}$" x 6$\frac{1}{2}$".

Fig 2

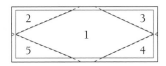

Making the Quilt Top

1. Place blocks in four rows of four blocks with sashing strips and 2$\frac{1}{2}$" squares in between.

continued next page

Approximate Size: 41" x 41"

Finished Block Size: 6" x 6" square

Materials

1 yd muslin (embroidered blocks)
1 yd tone on tone muslin print (sashing and second border)
1/4 yd each of 4 dk red prints (sashing)
3/4 yd dk red print (first border and binding)
1 1/2 yd backing fabric
batting
dk red embroidery floss

Cutting Requirements

16 - 8" squares, muslin (embroidered blocks)
40 - 2$\frac{1}{2}$" x 6$\frac{1}{2}$" rectangles, 10 each of four dk red prints (sashing)

80 - 1$\frac{3}{4}$" x 4$\frac{3}{8}$" rectangles, cut in half diagonally for 160 triangles, **Fig 1**, tone on tone muslin print (sashing)

Fig 1

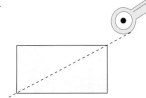

25 - 2$\frac{1}{2}$" squares, tone on tone muslin print (sashing squares)
four 1$\frac{1}{4}$"-wide strips, dk red print (first border)
four 3"-wide strips, tone on tone muslin print (second border)
four 2$\frac{1}{2}$"-wide strips, dk red print (binding)

Genteel Garden Quilt

2. Sew blocks to sashing strips; press seams towards blocks, **Fig 3.**

Fig 3

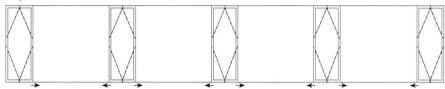

3. Sew sashing strips to squares; press seams towards squares, **Fig 4.**

Fig 4

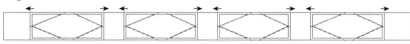

4. Sew sashing and block rows together.

5. Measure quilt top and add borders referring to Making the Quilt Top, page 61. Remove paper foundations at this time.

Finishing the Quilt

Refer to General Directions, pages 62 to 64, to mark, layer, quilt and bind your quilt. The photographed quilt was quilted in the ditch of sashing triangles and borders. The Star Quilting Pattern, below, was quilted randomly in the second border.

Foundation Pattern for Sashing Strip

Star Quilting Pattern

Weiss Women Crazy Quilt

Quilt Layout

Approximate Size:
21¹/₂" x 21¹/₂"

Finished Block Sizes:
7" square and 3¹/₂" square

Materials
³/₄ yd muslin (embroidered blocks and foundations)
assorted red print and solid scraps (blocks)
¹/₄ yd med red print (border)
¹/₈ yd dk red print (binding)
very thin batting, flannel, or fleece (optional)

red and off-white embroidery floss
assorted lace, seed beads, buttons and decorative crystal beads

Cutting Requirements
eight 8" squares, muslin (embroidered blocks and foundations)
eight 4¹/₂" squares, muslin (embroidered corner blocks and foundations)
four 4" x 14¹/₂" strips, med red print (border)
two 2¹/₂" x 21¹/₂" strips, med red print (binding)
two 2¹/₂" x 22¹/₂" strips, med red print (binding)

Embroidery Patterns
(pages 43 and 44)

Foundation Patterns
(pages 56 and 57)
Crazy Quilt Square
Crazy Quilt Corner Square

continued next page

Weiss Women Crazy Quilt

Instructions

Making the Blocks

1. Trace Embroidery patterns centered on the muslin squares. Trace Foundation patterns onto remaining muslin squares.

2. Embroider designs referring to Learn to do Redwork, pages 4 and 5.

3. Refer to Foundation Piecing, pages 59 to 61 to piece the blocks, **Fig 1.** Trim small blocks to 4" and large blocks to 7½", **Fig 2.**

Fig 1

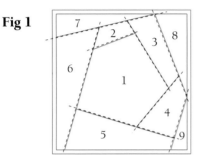

Fig 2

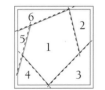

4. Embroider along seams using the Feather Stitch (page 5) and two strands of off-white floss, **Fig 3.** Substitute lace along a seam if desired. (See color photograph on back cover.)

Fig 3

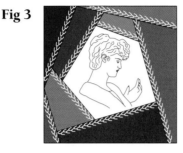

5. Add lace, beads and trims as desired.

Making the Quilt Top

1. Sew large blocks together in pairs, then sew pairs together.

2. Sew border strips to opposite sides of quilt top.

3. Sew a small block to each end of remaining border strips; sew to top and bottom of quilt, **Fig 4.**

Fig 4

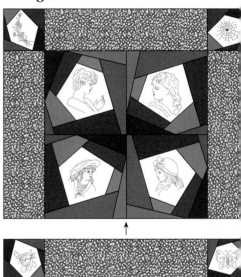

Crazy Quilt Corner Square

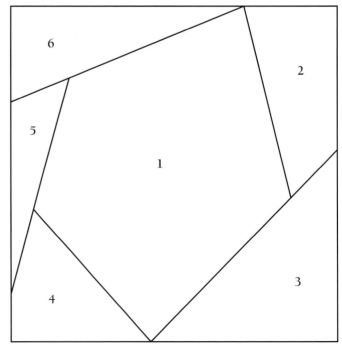

Finishing the Quilt
Refer to General Directions, pages 62
to 64, to finish your quilt. The photographed quilt was tacked at the corner of each block with buttons.

Crazy Quilt Square

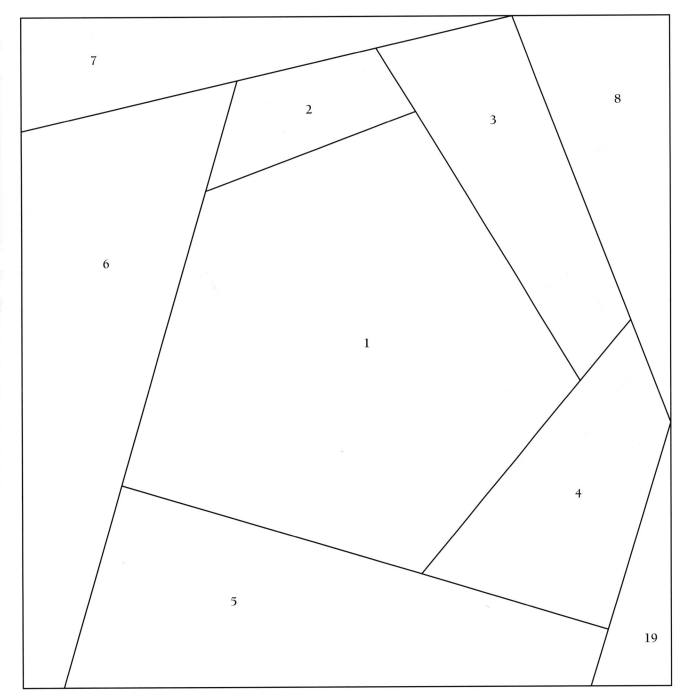

Ruffled Pillow

The pillow shown in color on the front cover, is a simple-to-make accessory for your Redwork quilt.

Materials
9" square muslin
four assorted red strips (2"-wide)
$3/8$ yd dk red print
$2^{1}/_2$ yds of $1^{1}/_2$"-wide flat lace
10" square backing fabric
polyester stuffing
3 yds thin cord or string

Instructions

Choose your favorite design (we used Baby with Mirror on page 45). Read Learn to Do Redwork, pages 4 and 5 for tracing and embroidery instructions and embroider design onto a 9" square of muslin. Trim block to 7" when finished.

1. Cut the following strips from assorted red fabrics:

> one 2" x 7"
> two 2" x $8^{1}/_2$"
> one 2" x 10"

2. Sew the strips to the block, log cabin style, beginning with the 2" x 7" strip. (See Making the Quilt Blocks in Ruby Red Log Cabin, pages 49 to 51, for instructions.) Press carefully.

3. To make ruffle, cut two crosswise strips, $6^{1}/_2$"-wide from dark red fabric. Sew short ends together to form a circle; press seams open, **Fig 1.**

Fig 1

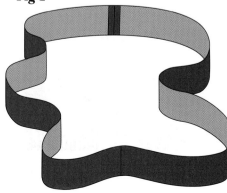

4. Fold in half lengthwise with wrong sides together; press, **Fig 2.**

Fig 2

5. Pin flat lace to one side of ruffle strip with straight edge of lace along raw edge of ruffle; baste in place if desired. This is the front side of the ruffle.

6. Sew gathering stitches along raw edge of back side of ruffle using a machine zigzag over a piece of string or cording, **Fig 3.** Be careful not to catch string in your stitching.

Fig 3

7. Place ruffle, lace side down on pillow front, with raw edges even and distributing gathers evenly, **Fig 4;** baste in place.

Fig 4

8. Place 10" backing square and embroidered block right sides together (ruffle will be sandwiched in between); pin or baste together. Stitch along three sides.

Turn right side out and check to see that ruffle did not get caught in stitching. If it did, remove stitching, adjust ruffle and restitch.

Stuff evenly with polyester stuffing.

Whipstitch open side closed.

General Directions

Foundation Piecing

Foundation piecing is the technique of sewing patchwork onto a foundation such as paper or fabric following a numerical sequence. It was used for two of the quilts, Genteel Garden Quilt (page 53) and Weiss Women Crazy Quilt (page 55).

Foundation Material

There are three popular options that can be used for foundations: fabric, paper or Tear-Away® interfacing.

A light-colored, lightweight cotton fabric or muslin are popular choices for crazy quilt blocks. They are light enough to see through to trace the pattern and they add extra stability to your blocks for the addition of trims, buttons and beads.

Paper is preferred by most quilters who do not want to have an extra layer of fabric in their quilts. Use any paper that you can see through (notebook paper, copy paper, newsprint or computer paper) for easy tracing, then tear it away after sewing is completed.

The new Tear-Away® interfacing is being used more and more. Like muslin, it is light enough to see through for tracing, but like paper, it can later be easily removed before quilting.

Preparing the Foundation

There are two methods for preparing the foundation: tracing and transferring.

TRACING THE BLOCK

Trace the block pattern carefully onto your chosen foundation material. Use a ruler and a fine-point permanent marker or fine-line mechanical pencil to make straight lines; be sure to include all numbers.

Draw a line ¼" from the outside edges of the block, **Fig 1;** cut along this outside drawn line. Repeat for the number of blocks needed for your quilt.

Fig 1

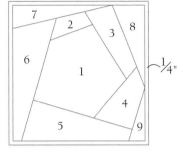

Remember, the finished block will be a mirror image of the pattern if the block is not symmetrical, **Fig 2.**

Fig 2

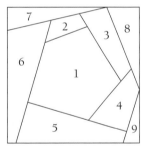

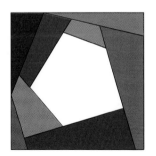

TRANSFERRING THE BLOCK

The block pattern can also be transferred onto foundation material, but to do this, involves an additional step if you want your block to look like the shaded diagram of the finished block. First, trace the block pattern onto tracing paper. Flop the paper so that the design is "backwards" and trace again onto plain paper using a transfer pen or pencil, **Fig 3.** Then, following manufacturer's directions, iron transferred design onto foundation material. If all these steps are not followed, your finished block will be a mirror image to the finished block, **Fig 4.**

Fig 3

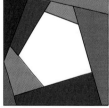

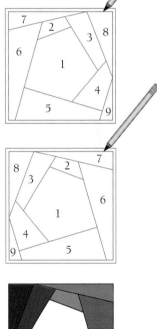

Fig 4

continued next page

General Directions

Cutting the Fabric

One of the main advantages to foundation piecing is that you do not have to cut every exact piece for every block. You can use strips, rectangles, squares or any odd-shaped scrap for piecing. You do have to be careful to use a piece of fabric that is at least 1/4" larger on all sides than the space it is to cover. Triangle shapes can be a little tricky to piece. Use generous-sized fabric pieces and be careful when positioning the pieces onto the foundation. You do waste some fabric this way, but the time it saves in cutting will be worth it in the end. In the Genteel Garden Quilt, we did give cutting instructions for the foundation-pieced sashing strips, but it is entirely optional as to whether you cut the pieces out ahead of time or not.

Making a Foundation-Pieced Block

Prepare foundations as described in Preparing the Foundation, page 59.

Turn the foundation with unmarked side facing you and position piece 1 over the space marked 1 on the foundation. Hold foundation up to a light source to make sure that fabric overlaps at least 1/4" on all sides of space 1, **Fig 5**; pin or use a glue stick to hold in place.

Fig 5

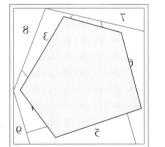

> **Hint:** Use only a small dab of a glue stick to hold fabric in place.

Place fabric piece 2 right sides together with piece 1. Double check to see if fabric piece chosen will cover space 2 completely by folding over along line between space 1 and 2, **Fig 6**.

Fig 6

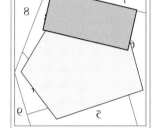

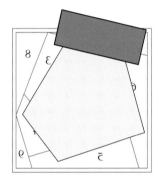

Turn foundation with marked side facing you and fold foundation forward along line between spaces 1 and 2; trim both pieces about 1/4" above fold, **Fig 7**. (You are actually pre-trimming the seam allowance of the first seam.)

Fig 7

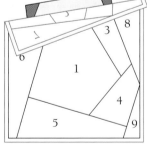

With marked side of foundation still facing you, position on sewing machine, holding fabric pieces in place. Sew along line between spaces 1 and 2 using a very small stitch (18 to 20 stitches per inch), **Fig 8**; begin and end sewing two to three stitches beyond line. You do not need to back stitch. If you are sewing on a fabric foundation, you can use a regular stitch length.

Fig 8

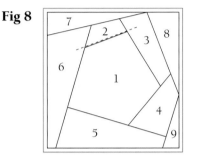

> **Hint:** Sewing with a very tiny stitch will allow for easier paper removal later. But, if paper falls apart right after stitching, your stitch length is too short and you will need to lengthen the stitch slightly.

Turn foundation over. Open piece 2 and finger press seam, **Fig 9**. Use a pin or dab of glue stick to hold piece in place if necessary.

Fig 9

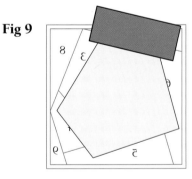

urn foundation with marked side of oundation facing you; fold foundaion forward along line between paces 2 and 3 and trim about 1/8" om fold, **Fig 10.**

ig 10

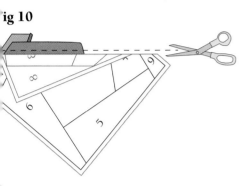

Note: Previous sewing may prevent foundation from being folded along just-sewn line.**:** If using a paper foundation, carefully pull paper away from stitching for easier trimming. If using a fabric foundation, fold it forward as far as it will go and trim.

lace fabric 3 right side down even ith just-trimmed edge, **Fig 11.**

ig 11

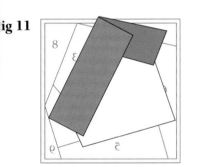

urn foundation to marked side and ew along line between spaces 2 and ; begin and end sewing 2 or 3 stitchs beyond line, **Fig 12.**

ig 12

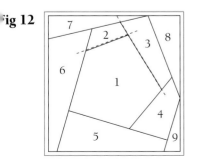

Turn foundation over, open piece 3 and finger press seam, **Fig 13.** Glue or pin in place.

Fig 13

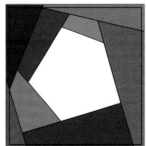

Continue trimming and sewing pieces in numerical order until block is complete, **Fig 14.** Make sure pieces along the outer edge are large enough to allow for the 1/4" seam allowance you drew around the block. Press block, them trim fabric even with outside line of foundation to complete block, **Fig 15.**

Fig 14

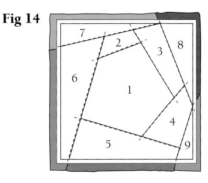

Fig 15

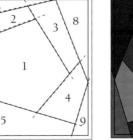

Hint: Do not remove paper at this time. It is better to remove paper after blocks have been sewn together. Since grain line wasn't considered in piecing, some of the outer edges may be on the bias and therefore, stretchy. Keeping the paper in place until after sewing will prevent the blocks from becoming distorted.

Finishing the Quilt

Making the Quilt Top

Sew quilt blocks together in rows unless specified otherwise. After sewing, press seams for rows in alternate directions to allow for easier piecing. Sew rows together, making sure to match seams.

Adding Borders

To add borders, measure quilt top lengthwise; cut two border strips to that length and sew to sides of quilt. If strips have to be pieced together to achieve desired length, sew together on the diagonal for a less noticeable seam line, **Fig 16.** Trim excess 1/4" from stitching.

Fig 16

continued next page

General Directions

Measure quilt top crosswise, including borders just added and cut two border strips to that length. Sew to top and bottom of quilt top. Repeat for any additional borders. Press after addition of each border.

If used, remove paper or non-woven backing at this time.

> **Hint:** Use tweezers to help remove paper from tiny areas.

Adding Borders with Mitered Corners

Borders with mitered corners take a little more work, but if you have a strip-pieced border like in Ruby Red Log Cabin, page 48, the final results will be worth the extra effort.

Measure quilt top lengthwise and crosswise; piece and cut border strips the lengthwise and crosswise measuremens of the quilt plus twice the width of the border and another $1/2$" for seam allowance. For example, if the length of your quilt is 80" and your border is 4" wide, cut side border strips 80" plus 8" (twice the border width) plus $1/2$" (seam allowance at each end) for a total of $88 1/2$".

Center the first border strip along edge of quilt top; be sure that there is a $4 1/4$" overlap (if the border will be 4" wide) at each end, **Fig 17.** If not, ease the quilt evenly into the border.

Fig 17

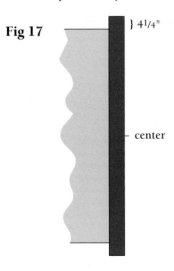

} $4 1/4$"

— center

Sew the border strip to the quilt, beginning and ending $1/4$" from each edge of the quilt top, **Fig 18;** backstitch at each end. Press.

Fig 18

Sew remaining border strips to quilt top in same manner.

To miter corners, fold the quilt in half diagonally with right sides together, matching edges of border, **Fig 19;** pin to keep border edges together, if necessary.

Fig 19

Place a ruler along the folded diagonal edge of quilt, extending ruler into border. Draw a diagonal line on border using a pencil or fabric pen, **Fig 20.**

Fig 20

Sew on drawn line going from the inner to the outer edge of border, **Fig 21.** Backstitch.

Fig 21

Open the quilt and check miter to make sure corner is square and flat.

Trim excess fabric $1/4$" from stitching **Fig 22;** press.

Fig 22

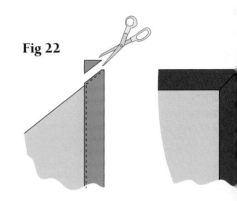

Repeat for remaining corners.

Marking the Quilt

Decide how you would like to quilt your quilt. If you are quilting "in the ditch" of the seam (the space right in the seam), marking is not necessary. If you are quilting around pieced shapes, you may not need to mark th lines if you feel you can accurately gauge the quilting line as you work. Any other quilting will need to be marked.